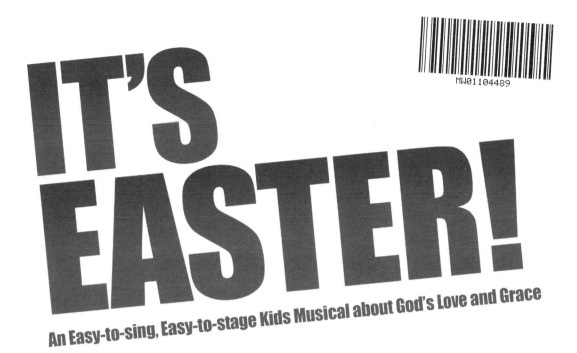

IT'S EASTER!

An Easy-to-sing, Easy-to-stage Kids Musical about God's Love and Grace

Compiled by **Cherry Garasi**

Contents

lillenas**kids**

2

When I Survey the Wondrous Cross

ISAAC WATTS

LOWELL MASON
Arranged by Steven V. Taylor

*CD POINTS: Split-channel, CD:1-4; Stereo Trax, CD:5-8

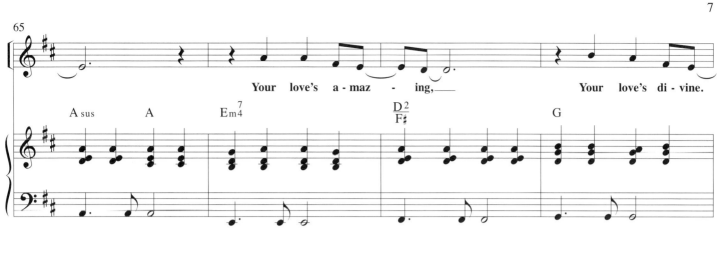

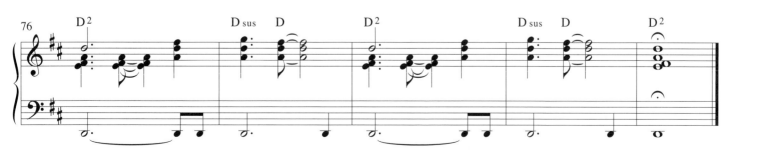

Nothing but the Blood

Words and Music by
ROBERT LOWRY
Arranged by Steven V. Taylor

Amazing Grace

JOHN NEWTON

Virginia Harmony, 1831
Arranged by Steven V. Taylor

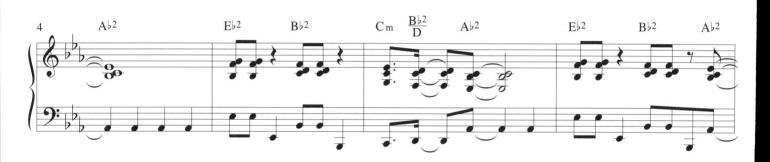

1st & 2nd times: CHOIR *unis.*
3rd time: SOLO

1. A - maz - ing grace! how
(2. 'Twas) grace that taught my
(3. When) we've been there ten

13

14

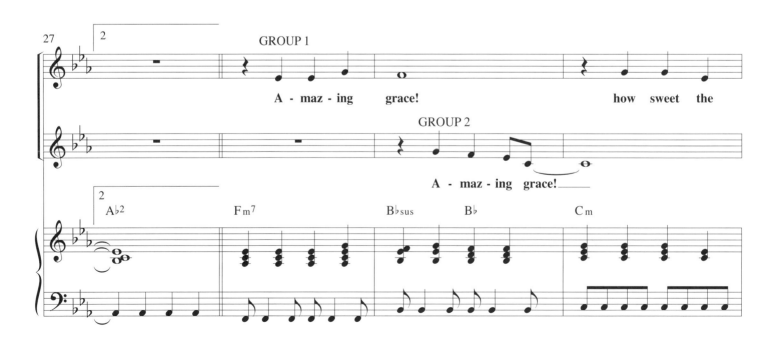

It's Easter

Words and Music by
PAM WALKER and
PAM ANDREWS
Arr. by John DeVries

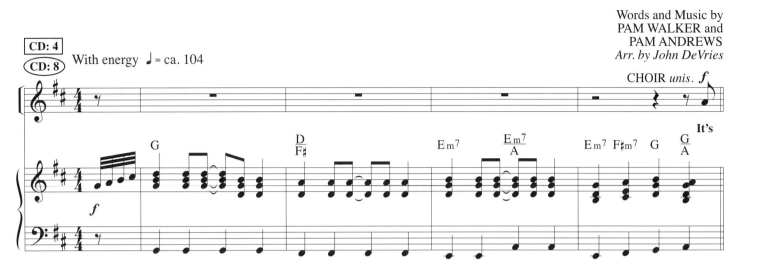

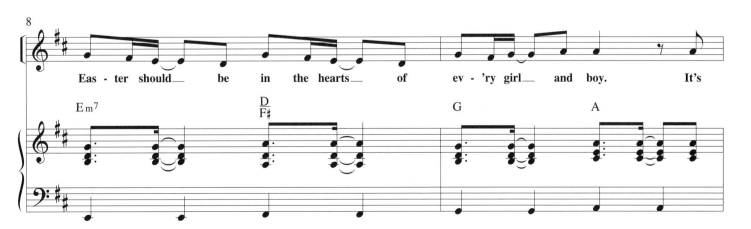

SCRIPT

This simple script of Bible verse and sentence speaking parts may be read by each speaker to simplify the preparation and rehearsal time for this musical.

Scene 1

(Stage Right. Three Readers exchange the following dialogue.)

READER #1: *(Adult leader)* It's Easter!

READER #2: *(Child)* Yes! Easter eggs, chocolate bunnies, new clothes . . .

READER #1: *(Adult leader)* Yes, those are the fun parts of Easter. But, Easter is really about Jesus' resurrection.

READER #2: *(Child)* Resurrection?

READER #1: *(Adult leader)* Yes, resurrection! We celebrate Easter because Christ rose from the grave. But, it all started at the cross . . .

(Scene changes to other side of stage where speakers quote the following scriptures before "When I Survey the Wondrous Cross".)

READER #4: "The people stood watching . . ." Luke 23:35

READER #5: "But all those who knew him, including the women who had followed him from Galilee, stood at a distance, watching these things." Luke 23:49

READER #6: "But God demonstrates his own love for us in this: While we were still sinners, Christ died for us." Romans 5:8

Song #1 - WHEN I SURVEY THE WONDROUS CROSS

Scene 2

(Readers read the following scripture to set up Song #2, "Nothing but the Blood".)

READER #7: "In him we have redemption through his blood, the forgiveness for sins, in accordance with the riches of God's grace . . ." Ephesians 1:7

READER #8: "If we claim to be without sin, we deceive ourselves and the truth is not in us." 1 John 1:8

Song #2 - NOTHING BUT THE BLOOD

Scene 3

(Speakers read the following scripture to set up Song #3, "Amazing Grace".)

READER #9: "For it is by grace you have been saved, through faith - and this not from yourselves, it is the gift of God - not by works, so that no one can boast." Ephesians 2:8-9

READER #10: "Jesus answered, 'I am the way and the truth and the life. No one comes to the Father except through me.'" John 14:6

Song #3 - AMAZING GRACE

Scene 4

(Scripture and dialogue set up Song #4, "It's Easter!")

READER #11: *(Adult leader)* Easter is all about God's love for us!

(READER #12 moves to front center stage and quotes John 3:16 from memory.)

READER #12: "For God so loved the world that He gave His one and only Son, that whoever believes in him shall not perish but have eternal life." John 3:16

Song #4 - IT'S EASTER!

Production Notes and Performance Suggestions

• Each song can be performed as a single song and the related scripture can be shared prior to singing in all kinds of worship settings. You may choose to have the children sing one of the hymn arrangements for each of the three Sundays of Lent and then sing, "It's Easter!" on Easter Sunday morning.

• Accompaniment Tracks may be used for each song, providing support and excitement to young singer's performance.

• Print each reading on a cross (approx. 12 inches high) made from construction paper or heavy card stock and have the readers hold them toward the audience as they read their lines. The crosses can be glued or taped to short dowel rods so they can be held by the reader.

• Have the audience or congregation join the children in singing, "Amazing Grace" to provide a joint worship experience for everyone.

• Use whatever lighting you may have in your particular venue to enhance the performance. Spotlight speakers and readers. Use dimmer lighting for the songs about the cross, and use brighter and colored lighting for "It's Easter!"

• Work with your pastor and staff to incorporate the performance of these songs into your services at Easter and during Lent to provide opportunities for your children to lead in worship.

• Go to a retirement home or have your children share this musical at a senior adult meeting or function around Easter time. Seniors will enjoy a "sing-a-long" of the hymns and will be delighted to hear children reciting the scripture verses.

• Be creative in your production. Use creative persons in your church or school to create videos that might accompany the songs in this musical. Have volunteers bring flowers and palms to decorate the stage when you sing. Display a large cross on one side of the stage for your production. Drape it with purple or white cloth as the musical progresses.